Passive Income Pathway

LEGAL NOTICES

PASSIVE INCOME PATHWAY

TESTED, TRUSTED, RISK-FREE
WAY TO FINANCIAL FREEDOM

Kenneth Ejiofor

WARNING!

Before you proceed to read this book, visit www.kennethejiofor.acnshop.eu

That is when the content will make any sense to you. Play around with the flags at the bottom of the page by clicking on each one. You will be amazed how technology has made online business easier than you have ever imagined.

The website is hosted and managed for free. When you become part of the business, you will become a global player by owning your own free business website where you can connect with all the listed countries and be a licensed partner to market all listed products and services.

Do not forget to come back and complete the reading of the Book.

See you!

GET IN TOUCH

Visit www.kennethejiofor.acnshop.eu

Click on the email or phone sign under my Business ID for enquiry

Books by Kenneth Ejiofor available on www.amazon.com are:

The Divided Church: An Irony of the truth

Do Not Lose Your Friends: A Practical Guide to Sustaining Relationships.

Passive Income Pathway: Tested, Trusted, Risk-Free Way to Financial Freedom

TABLE OF CONTENTS

WHY I WROTE THIS BOOK

I know that there are millions of young minds who have been in the quest of trying to be financially free; persons who have read a lot of financial breakthrough books and success motivated books but have never been able to break free from the circle of normal work life because they have not been able to meet their financial obligations which only passive income can provide. Some have embarked on different forms of private businesses but have failed because of the risk many new businesses face and the huge task of competing with already established ones.

However, when I came to the full understanding of this financially liberating business idea (making money while asleep) that has set me on a pedestal of financial freedom, I said to myself: "Ken, more people need to hear this". The reason for this is that this business idea I want to share with you is a business that is already sweeping across the globe with a lot of beneficiaries.

How To get involved

After reading this book and discover that you are one of those persons like me who have been looking for a way out, get in touch through the website www.kennethejiofor.acnshop.eu Click on the email or phone sign under my Business ID for enquiry

Please refer to the list of Countries on the website to know if you are eligible to join this business currently. If your country flag is not on the list, keep an eye on the website as more countries join. I also recommend you introduce this book to your friends and family members who are currently residing in any of the named countries so they can exploit the opportunity and enjoy financial freedom.

CHAPTER ONE

INTRODUCTION

I have attended a lot of financial freedom seminars of which other attendees and I often get so excited about the principles that we saw worked for the presenters and how far they have gone in achieving great success and thus, we often feel we can get to a higher level, or at least to that same level of the presenters. Nonetheless, most times, we count the cost of getting to those levels right at the event and we go home more miserable than we came. Do I have a witness out there? Sure, I know you are there! The most frustrating part of it all is when you courageously attend some of these 'secret of making money events', with a significant percentage of your insignificant income as a result of the event's first advert which promised that by attending the event, you will be a financial master-planner who is free from work or financial stress. Then at the end of the event or after each speaker comes up to tell you how you could make thousands of dollars in a month, you are requested to pay more to get deeper revelation on how to use these principles. Most times it doesn't end there. If you are privileged to have some more resources and put them in to attend the second phase, there is sure another third phase to attend on a higher rate that you never envisaged when you signed up for the first event. Imagine the first advert stated just 100 dollars to your financial freedom. You jumped at it thinking you would be free from financial troubles. Thereafter, they told you that to get into the phase where you will get personal tools to unlock your fortunes, you needed to register for another phase with a thousand dollar. As usual, over 80 percent of the participant will definitely drop out at this stage. Then peradventure you are one of the 20 percent who are privileged to afford the fees for the next stage, you must have thought and said, "yea, my little savings which I was able to save in twelve months or more is just a little above a thousand dollars, I can take this out and attend as far as I am getting out of this financial mess". There you go! You registered with great hope and expectations. The day for the awaited seminar finally came and you said to yourself, "it is time to settle this once and for all". Yes, the event was great and quite revealing. Suddenly you hear "I want just a handful of you here that I will personally mentor and ensure you are never going to work for money again". This time, the registration fee is $10,000 or more. You end up being so frustrated and wishing you never started the course at all. It is the same thing with books. You may have read countless numbers of books to gain financial freedom but has not been able to implement one of them. You can tell everyone how to make money due to the knowledge you have gained from the numerous books you have read but you are not making money. You are still as wretched or more wretched than when you started reading these books. The Principles are so awesome but when you step out to put them into practice you discovered that they were not as easy as they were stated in the books. Again, you close up the books and continue with your normal life. The financial freedom you have envisaged becomes an illusion.

Is there anything wrong in attending numerous financial breakthrough events or reading more books about money? No! The best investment anyone can still make in life is investing in your personal development in any area you desired changes because no knowledge is ever lost. I have attended a lot of those courses and events, read numerous financial freedom books, that is why I have the knowledge of what I am sharing with you in this book. The truth is that for you to decide to attend a cheap financial freedom event or buy and read books for same purpose shows that you desire change. The fact that you are reading this book at this moment is also a great indication that you want to secure a future for yourself and subsequent generations. Most times, what we need to scale through financial huddles is someone or a group of business professionals ready to take you through. That is the purpose of this book. It is worth stating here that today, my books are selling on Amazon worldwide because I met people who guided me through publishing on Amazon and I have also helped others to publish their books. You can check out my Books on Amazon on the 'get in touch' and back cover page of this book.

With this opportunity before you, the problem is not going to be capital but your ability to work with a team, ready to learn and implement tested and proven principles to grow your business.

CHAPTER TWO

THE DIMENSION OR TREND OF SALES IN THE WORLD TODAY (STAYING CURRENT)

Any one who desire to be financially free must stay current with the happenings in the financial and business world. If you are getting ready to explore the world of the rich today and still cannot surf the internet for opportunities, it is obvious that you are not yet ready to be financially free. Recently, in the United Kingdom, several thriving popular shops have announced closure of so many of their branches. You may have heard of those big names shutting down sales outlets and you wonder what had happened to them because they seemed to be so well established that one may think that they can never go bankrupt. The most recent ones are banks shutting down hundreds of retail outlets all over the country for same reason. As it is happening here, so it is all over the world especially the developed nations of the world. The developing nations are not left out as knowledge and technology increases.

Are you still imagining what has gone wrong with the big names that are shutting down? It is very simple. Online shoppers are taking over physical shopping and thus millions will be losing their jobs worldwide due to the closure of these former known employers of labour. Also, getting jobs has become very hard because the available spots for people are drastically reducing daily.

One thing I want you to register in your heart at this point is that consumption of these goods has not reduced in anyway. Infact, demand for them are on the increase because population is on the increase daily and with the online shopping, purchasing power of consumers is higher. The simple logic behind the purchasing power of buyers increasing is that online products tend to be cheaper compared to their prices in shops and this is simply because the cost of maintaining the physical shops are added to the price of the goods sold in there. The removal of that retail store interface has therefore reduced the cost of the products as most goods can now go directly from the producers to the consumers due to online shopping.

Let the wise apply wisdom, it is time to dream big.

CHAPTER THREE

THE DREAM

When the leading shops are closing down outlets due to increase in online shopping, the wise will begin to look at how they can take advantage of the new trend to be financially free through passive income. Passive income is when you do a thing once, but you are getting paid for it for a long duration of time or possibly being paid for it in a lifetime. This is the dream! While you are sleeping, money is still coming into your account because someone somewhere is using what he or she has been using, and something they cannot do without.

Dreaming it is the starting stage of being financially free. If you haven't dreamt about it before, this is the right time to begin to dream it because it is possible. Just as online shopping has become and is further becoming increasingly simple, so has it become much more simple for you to gain financial freedom doing this business via online contact and physical contact to gain so much that you will never have to work for someone again. Remember, if it is not something you do once and keep reaping its profit, it is not called residual income. Financial freedom means that you can literally go to sleep, and your income will still be flowing in and increasing steadily. Is this your dream?

I remember when I was being introduced into this life changing opportunity business, one question my mentor asked me was; "What is your motivating factor for seeking financial freedom"? This is a question you must answer right away that will position you better to take up this opportunity and to pursue it with the whole of your heart. If one of your dream is to be free from the rat race of eight or nine hours work time a day, how have you planned to achieve it? If your dream is to travel the world and be free to do it at any time all over again, how have you planned to achieve it? If your dream is to have more time for your family and friends, how have you planned to achieve it? What is your dream?

A young man once told me that his motivating dream for seeking financial freedom was to lessen the burden for his mum who was a single parent toiling day and night to see that him and his three siblings are well taken care of.

Once you have identified the dream, how to achieve it is the next step. No matter what your dream is, as far as it has to do with money, I can assure you this is a good start for you. From here, you will be able to set up other businesses that you have always dreamt about because you will be sure of residual income. In addition, you will have more time to focus on building your life and future instead of working for others. The dream is very important, but it is not enough to dream. The very step you take towards achieving the dream is far more important.

CHAPTER FOUR

TAKING THE STEP

Taking the step starts with your understanding of residual or passive income and what it means to you and your dream. Thus, the freedom and the time it provides for you to be able to get other things in place cannot be overemphasised. If you are a big dreamer, you need residual income.

Once you have settled this in your mind and you know that you have not been able to get a way out before now, or you need an extra more of residual income which can grow eventually, this is your opportunity to take the right step in getting in touch with the author through the website and start up right away. Your start up capital is simply your license fee, but I can assure you that it will not be a burden to you. It cannot be compared to the situation where you have to save or borrow so much to start up a business on your own.

This is the point that is so hard for new people especially the young in business when they have to save so much to start up a business they never know when its products or services would be accepted or sold enough to breakeven and thus profit them.

According to the Small Business Association (SBA), It is on record that Thirty percent (30%) of new businesses fail during the first two years of being open, Fifty percent (50%) during the first five years and Sixty Six percent (66%) during the first ten years. You can read up the reasons this happens on the internet by using google search engine. This is why many young entrepreneurs find it hard to start up something because of the uncertainty ahead and that is why I am writing this book to bring the awareness to millions of people who have always dreamt of owning and making profits in their own businesses as this business is devoid of such uncertainties. You are literally partnering with established companies who will be working for you and not you work for them. In your enquiry, ask me How.

CHAPTER FIVE

THE SUPPORT

The lack of the right support from people who have already mastered the act in a particular business is one major challenge that most new businesses suffer which eventually leads to them closing down too soon. Many established businesses always see others in same line as threat if they don't do the needful to hinder the new ones from coming up. This is quite the opposite in this case as the growth of others with you means that you are growing too. There is no competition in the system, we are complimentary to one another. The business has been so structured that in any of the countries where you sign up, you are not left alone. Already established team members are there to guide you through until you become well established. There are a lot of workshops/seminars both local and international that will give you all that you need to know at all point to ensure that you become a professional in no time.

The website is a well-structured platform that gives you all tools that you need to be the best in your business. You are open to twenty-four hours support system that help you trace and monitor your progress, get on hand advice at each time you need it in your personal online office which becomes accessible when you sign up. It is like carrying your office wherever you go.

The support is amazing.

All these are hosted and managed for you free of charge. You don't need to worry about the cost of maintaining it. Booking a zoom call, you can see details of what your online office looks like.

CHAPTER SIX

THE RISK ASSOCIATED IN YOUR OWN BUSINESS

The fear of the risks associated with starting up a new business in the face of so many big names that already exist in the market has kept so many people in their static financial state. However, these dreaded risks have been taken care of because we are partnering with already established and well-known companies. In each of the listed countries on the website, you will see a host of trusted companies that you will be partnering with. You will quite agree with me that brand matters a lot in deciding what consumers buy, that is why you can go to sleep with your two eyes closed while these great brands all over the world work for you.

CHAPTER SEVEN

GROWTH

The business is designed in a way that everyone has the opportunity to grow. Overtaking is also allowed in the sense that hard work always pays off. This means that the more time you commit to it, the more gain you make. Just as a plant that is well tended will do better than that which is left alone among weeds, so is your commitment to your business. As an international business owner, your coast is everywhere the company is registered. This is where you take advantage of the global internet and online marketing to grow without boundary. You don't need to be on ground to meet your prospective customers, your personal online shop (the website) is all you need to move around each country from the comfort of your home.

CHAPTER EIGHT

YOUR COAST

You will agree with me that the available market for any product is one of the major determinants of the growth of the business. Here you are being introduced to a business whose products are essential everyday products and services which people cannot do without and you have the world to market from the comfort of your house. The book in your hands gives you that advantage to be a member of a team working together to grow together. Currently, the business is in over 26 countries which are listed below and still growing. I call it a wave that is sweeping across the world. I see it taking over in every nation as technology advances globally. That means that you will always have the market you need. Listed below are the countries where you can currently trade without having to travel there. If your country of residence is already connected, I want to specially congratulate you because your new dawn has begun. However, if your country is not yet listed, look out for it because we are coming to you sooner than you expect.

Here is our trading coast as at the time of publishing this book

1. Austria
2. Australia
3. Belgium
4. Canada
5. Colombia
6. Czech Republic
7. Denmark
8. Finland
9. France
10. Germany
11. Hungary
12. Ireland
13. Italy
14. Japan
15. Mexico
16. Netherlands
17. New Zealand
18. Norway

19.Peru

20.Poland

21.Portugal

22.South Korea

23.Spain

24.Sweden

25.Switzerland

26.United Kingdom

27.United State

Visit www.kennethejiofor.acnshop.eu to have up to date list of countries

CHAPTER NINE

THE PERSONALITY GAIN

Though you may expect me to say that the most beautiful thing about this business is the income which keeps coming even when I am asleep, I am sorry to disappoint you because for me, the area I enjoy most is the kind of personalities I have come to know and associate with. The people you work with or the company you keep defines who you truly are, and it has great potential to remold and refine you. There is nothing as beautiful as building a network with people who you know are pushing to make great impact in the world. One good thing about relating with people of such great vision is that their life and vision rub off on you. In no distant time, you will see yourself talking like them, doing things and going to places like them. The wealth and influence will follow because you are in connection with wealthy and influential personalities. It starts with you going back to 'get in touch' page. Partnering with a world class company makes you a world class person, not just because you are working with them but because you are achieving similar results of which I am certain that you will achieve. Imagine when you tell prospective customers that you are trading in almost thirty countries around the world. How awesome it is knowing that you joined a business today and you already have a platform where you can market and sell products and services to people in about 30 countries and still growing. It is such an amazing opportunity that you will never want to lose.

Dare to become an international personality! Join the league of people with the vision to conquer the world with their wealth.

CHAPTER TEN

WEALTH SUSTENANCE

The best type of wealth any foresighted individual must be involved in is that which will transcend his generation. That is the kind of wealth that your children and children's children will inherit. That is why some family in this world will hardly go back to poverty because they have such a business that keep fetching in so much that even when the starter has long gone, the children are still enjoying it.

When you finally start up this business, you will not only be doing yourself good but up to your unborn generation. Signing up makes it your own business which you have the right to transfer to anyone you wish to. This is a characteristic which makes the wealth gain in it a sustainable one. Surely, this business will become one that you must state in your will one day. "A good man leaves an inheritance for his children's children" says the Holy Bible. A good man will always think generationally. Be good!

CHAPTER ELEVEN

THE BUSINESS

The business is to partner and promote home essential services to people while you get paid over and over again as long as they continue to use the products and services. That means, the company takes over the care of the customers but keep paying you. You will be trained on the simple techniques for marketing the products and how you can recruit others to join your team. The first fear that grips new business people is the issue of acceptance in the market because it is very hard to get people to test and use new products, but in this case, you are not introducing a new product or service to your customers. Rather, you are selling to them what they are already using with cheaper and more secured deals. Note that I did not say 'what they may be probably using' because they are products and services that they cannot do without (see my online shop; www.kennethejiofor.acnshop.eu). One thing everyone always look out for is an opportunity to save some money no matter how small. This platform will help you to secure deals for family and friends to save some money monthly on their spending on essential services and products. This has completely eradicated the fear of acceptance because you will be helping your customers to save money. They will not only come back to thank you but will be glad to introduce their friends and families for you to help them as well because you have put smile on their face. Thus, the more people you help to smile, the more you are smiling with your account. It is a win-win deal.

CHAPTER TWELVE

CUSTOMERS ACQUISITION

Acquiring customer is easy. The first customer you get is you because you are already using and paying for the services. Instead of just paying for the service as you have been doing before starting up this business, this time, you will start earning points and residual income for using the very same products and services you have been using. Next is to get others in your sphere of contact to switch to your service providers. These include family and friends who are already using same products and services too. Now, you will start getting paid for their bills too. Also, using the power of the internet through all the social media platforms, you can always get more. People will always patronise you when they know you are out to help them too. It is a win-win business because you help them reduce their spending with a more efficient service and you gain by acquiring residual income.

Joining the business is a sign that you want to be free from the usual rat race life of many average people on the street. It is a signal that you know what residual income is, and you want to enjoy it whereby even when you are travelling round the world or sleeping, money is coming into your account because someone is paying for what they cannot do without. It is that beautiful. You can also get your business expanded by bringing in people to join the business from all over the world.

The most beautiful aspect of this opportunity is when you build your network. That is where your efforts become working smart and not working hard. In that instance, you will be in your country and as people use their essential services all over the places where your network is, you are constantly earning money. So, you earn money from your immediate customers and from your network. You can never know how far your business network can spread because someone always know someone that knows someone. It goes on and on and on.

To build your network from the comfort of your house leveraging on the internet, you can get someone you know or a total stranger far away in another country to sign up into this business and from that point, you begin to recruit more person into your network. It will no longer be only you that is getting people into the network but also those you have brought in who will be bringing in others and that is how you recruit more person and your network will keep expanding. Those who sign up becomes your recruits that will help in the expansion of the network that you are building. The list is endless.

CHAPTER THIRTEEN

CONCLUSION: THE FREEDOM

The conclusion of it all is that every man or woman who desires a good life wants to be free and this includes freedom from the usual and most common lifestyle of the average man or woman on the street who is tied to the daily routine of eight or nine hours work time. The man or woman with a vision will want to escape that scenario where you are forced to come to work not minding if the weather is favourable or not; your boss will never want to hear that, because you must work for your money. The truth is that everyone desires this freedom. While some persons are working tirelessly to achieve it, some feel it is better to remain in that seemingly comfort zone. You will think it is a comfort zone until the day you are handed a sack letter. I know that there are some persons who have tried their best to be free but have resigned to fate because of the task of getting free, but here is your freedom at last. Get in touch, get started now.

About the Author

Kenneth Ejiofor is a writer and best seller author whose books have impacted many lives across the globe. He is a successful entrepreneur who enjoys showing others the way as he has enjoyed same from his circle of friends. He is a distinguished relationship counsellor who believe so much in the power of friendship when well harnessed. Having enjoyed so much from friends who have in one time or the other showed him the path to success, he wrote and published his first book which he titled 'Do Not Lose your Friends: A practical guide to sustaining relationships'. He later went ahead to write about the unity in Christianity in his book 'The Divided Church: An irony of the truth'. He is a *Youtuber* where he talks about the power of love. He lives in the United Kingdom with his wife Esther and their daughter Royale.

About the Book

This book will launch you into financial freedom

It will link you up with others with similar desire to be different

It will guide you to generational wealth which you can leave for your children's children

Joining the team this book presents will make you an international marketer from the comfort of your house.

Read it, join the team, implement the plan, live the life you have always wanted.